Betty Hogan Cannella

Dec 4/04

A Sudden Sky

Ulrikka S. Gernes
A Sudden Sky
Selected Poems

translated and edited by
Patrick Friesen and Per Brask

Brick Books

NATIONAL LIBRARY OF CANADA CATALOGUING IN PUBLICATION DATA

Gernes, Ulrikka S.
A sudden sky : selected poems

ISBN 1-894078-18-7

I. Friesen, Patrick, 1946– . II. Brask, Per K., 1952– .
III. Title.

PT8176.17.E72A24 2001   839.8'II74   C2001-930382-3

Copyright © Ulrikka S. Gernes, 2001.

We acknowledge the support of the Canada Council for
the Arts for our publishing programme. The support of the
Ontario Arts Council is also gratefully acknowledged.

The publisher acknowledges the support of the Danish
Literature Information Centre for translation costs and the
translators are grateful to the Danish Literary Council for
travel support.

The cover photographs and design are by Marijke Friesen.

Typeset in Bauer Bodoni; the stock is Zephyr Antique laid.

Brick Books
431 Boler Road, Box 20081
London, Ontario N6K 4G6

brick.books@sympatico.ca

Contents

Foreword   9

from Natsværmer (Moth, 1984)

Eternity   13
In the Shadow of a Dream   14
Don't Speak of Dust and Roses   15
Blue Morning   16
Elegy   17
Trilobite   19
Leaf Fall   20
Metamorphoses   21
Memories Fade   22
Black Birds Liberate the Wind   23
Black Skies   24

from Englekløer (Angel Claws, 1985)

These Days   27
You Kneel   29
Found on the Beach   30
On Waiting   31
In the Park   32
Black Shadow   33
At the Window   34
October's Bridges   35
I have a blue mountain chain   36

from Hjortehjerte (Deer Heart, 1987)

Silk   41
November   42

Scar   43
I Came Here to Find You   44
The Watery Globe   45

from Skriftsteder (Scriptures, 1989)

faces in the crowd ...   49
the water under the stars ...   50
whom you dream into ...   51
for a moment I'm forgotten ...   52
without a single word ...   53
for nothing ...   54

from At (To, 1990)

to walk in a circle ...   57
to appear ...   58
to balance above fear ...   59

from Gribbenes Himmel (Vultures' Sky, 1993)

The Stranger   63
Moon Nail   64
Mad Bird   66
Grandmother   67
Carrying Sorrow   68
Not a Poem   70
Hotel   71
Exile   73
Sloughing   75
Travel   76

from Til (For, 1995)

Imploding Sky   79
The Witness   80
Entreaty   81
Thaw   82
Photography   83
In the Old City   84
In the Desert   85
Days   86

from Kamikaze (1999)

The Moon Knows …   89
I Refuse to accept …   91
You Know Those Nights …   92
If I Say that white horses …   93
Your Name Is Written …   94
From Now On I will always …   95

New Poems

Birthday at the Assistens Cemetery   99
The Pattern of Dead Insects   102
The Cannibals   104

Author Biography   109
Translators' Biographies   111

Foreword

Ulrikka S. Gernes was born at Ängelholm, in the province of Scania, in Sweden in 1965, of Danish parents. Her father was the internationally known visual artist Poul Gernes.

At the age of twenty-two she moved to Copenhagen, Denmark, already a published and highly acclaimed poet. Her first collection, *Natsværmer* [Moth], was published in Denmark in 1984, when she was eighteen years old. Since then she has published an additional eight collections, all of them received gratefully in the Danish press.

She has called poetry 'a resistance movement,' explaining that 'A poem's language contains a power which moves against the language of officialdom, the language of the media and the politicians, the language of commerce. A poem gives us the possibility of hearing our own voices. While the media offers us the world in small pieces, which are experienced as chaos, poetry seeks connections.'

Gernes also seeks to express the inner worlds of love, distance and the experience of nature. There is a beautiful neo-romantic streak in her work, as if the poet were seeking the language which would reveal and express the interconnectedness of all things. Says Liselotte Wiemer in a review of Gernes's most recent book, *Kamikaze,* in *Berlingske Tidende,* one of Denmark's most influential newspapers, 'These poems were written with the very tips of the fingers and the innermost threads of life. Sometimes, the writing is so blindingly beautiful that it is almost unbearable.'

We first came across Ulrikka Gernes when, several years ago, we were considering poems for a planned anthology of Danish poetry. Gernes was living in Hong Kong at the time, as she did on and off for many years during the 1990s. As we were preparing our translation and seeking her advice, it became clear that we were working with a poet of rare insight into process and languages. Over the years we translated an increasing number of her poems.

When Gernes read at the Vancouver Writers Festival in 1997, it became abundantly clear that her work found a true resonance with her first Canadian audience. Don McKay, of Brick Books, expressed an interest in seeing a collection, and we began the work of selecting the poems from Gernes's entire production which we thought could best be rendered in English through our particular sensibilities.

Gernes suggested a list of her poems, as did we, and between the two lists we eventually came to the current collection. Our aim in our selection was to give an indication of the sweep and evolution of the poet while, at the same time, choosing those poems we felt would work well in translation. We would arrive at our translations by Brask first sketching a rough translation which he would send to Friesen. Friesen would work on this sketch and would return it to Brask who would adjust and tweak this draft against what he deemed possible viz the original Danish. This process would continue for each poem until both Friesen and Brask felt satisfied with the result.

In the summer of 2000 we went to Copenhagen to meet with Gernes, whose English is exceptionally good. Here the three of us worked through every poem, with Gernes on several occasions rewriting lines, eventually arriving at the renderings before you. The process of bringing this book into being has been artistically rigorous, demanding and deeply fulfilling. It is with a sense of true delight that we put before Canadian poetry readers this first-rate Danish poet.

We would like to thank the Danish Literature Information Centre for its support of our work and the Danish Literature Council for supporting our trip to Denmark.

Patrick Friesen and *Per Brask*,
Vancouver and Winnipeg

**from Natsværmer
(Moth, 1984)**

Eternity

Stillness and the dark
hold my head
in their soft hands

I listen for a whisper
that carries silence
through the night

Wild birds of darkness answer
blinded by the light
in their eyes
dust and solitude
count the four walls
over and over again

In the Shadow of a Dream

Imagine being found
on a morning like this
in the fragrance of spring rain
every sense a painful
happiness breathing
on a morning like this
a little lonely a little dazed
eyes still filled
with longing and dreams

To see you walk through
a veil of fog and gates of rain
to meet me this morning
with a glance that says
that I am seen and found
for as long as forever

Don't Speak of Dust and Roses

Don't speak of dust and roses
or anything perishable
Don't speak of rain from a clear sky
or birds in cages of air
The moon remembers moments
luminous seconds of stillness
when we were perfect
Man and Woman
King and Queen
like dolphins in the ocean
we glided into
thin and wild embraces
Don't speak of lost dreams
each arrival another exit
Don't forget the poems
behind all that you know
behind all that you want
Here's a rainbow for your hair
Here's a wind that sings of love
Here all fairy tales come true
Look – I lift the Moon
from the ocean's wild mirror

Blue Morning

I will take you along
into the blue morning
shattering ice
against our window
I will take you along
and show you
the white wild birds
silently rising
from night's dreams
I will show you
that nothing is changed
but everything is different
today
since we've been given
such beautiful wings
So come along my Love
into the blue morning
and let us leave the Earth
on the wings of those dreams
through November's landscape

Elegy

However heavy the hand grows
that lifts the glass from the table
however trembling the lip
we belong to each other

Into the world
beneath birds beating against the wind
however difficult the steps
however wet the cheek
however blinded the eye
from longing and sorrow
we belong to each other

However little the words say
however loud the heart screams
in my dark breast
however empty the soul feels
from distances and departures
we belong to each other

In someone else's arms
however much tenderness and caresses hurt
how difficult to love another
with your face
etched into my eye's rainbow film
we belong to each other

Much is left to live with and through
Many days many nights
sun and moon forever shifting
much is left to love and hate
many seasons many strange places
are calling
However heavy my hand will grow
in frantic search for yours
we belong to each other

Trilobite

The sign of love
glimpses and flakes of solitude
tears departure or flight
all the things that are to happen
in our lives
all wanderings in the dark
along endless alleys of thought
are already determined
In the smallest details
the trails are etched
across the map

All our lives
and Everything
is written
within the blind letters of fossils
this undeniable structure
on which everything rests
Nowhere can we escape
silence's net of veins
Imprints of life

Leaf Fall

Leaves yellow
and fall from trees
covering the ground like poems
striped by rain
You and I
we see them
and read lines from heaven's blue story
thin as skin

We recognize the messages
beating in Earth's pulse
remembering into
these secret capillaries

We recognize
in mute wonder
and we understand

Metamorphoses

The sun dies
like a swan of light
Birds extinguish their lightning
through the air
towards evening
Flowers fall asleep
softly leaning against the dark
Windows stare
into nothing

Half thinking
I lift my hand now and again
and caress
night's dense plumage
In the arms of sleep
fishes begin to speak
about the brevity of all things
and dreams kiss each other
passionately
in the land behind all borders

Memories Fade

I think of you now
as a dream I had
under wings of glass
in a kingdom
lost in the roving of time
In the evening's
darkening forest
a place no one knows
where the bow maker
braids a string from your hair
I see you
bring him bread and wine

Down through years
deeds and ruins
that had to happen
black-shadowed creatures
conquered your realm and tied you
to their will
Your knights rode off
on the wind
Memories fade
in the evening's
darkening forest
a place no one knows
Only an arrow that didn't know its way
and a broken string are left behind
You grasp them
in your hand

Black Birds Liberate the Wind

Black birds liberate the wind
while softly diving
silent and blind
toward the shafts of the underground

I stand staring
from a broken window
ruins far from life and noise
where eyes grow bat wings
over endless landscapes
smelling of soot and ashes

Lonely my thought follows
the last glimpse of my presence
into the alleys of dreams beyond
bridges of glass and pollen
between miracles and wonders
all places that do not exist
and can never be destroyed

Black Skies

Today
light sinks
like stones
toward the bottom of the eye

Pain and happiness
are two colours
fused
in the rain

I cry
my forehead
has taken root
in this dense darkness

from Englekløer
(Angel Claws, 1985)

These Days

We shall live these days, my Love
    with blue trees, angels and wine
    while the beaches are forgotten
    and the wind blows away laughter

We shall live these days, my Love
    in increasing loneliness
    empty streets, together
    friends leave, migratory birds
    in huge black flocks
    we shall live here
    holding silence in our hands

The nights filled with long caresses
that keep the dreams awake
and make the skin soft and warm under cover of the dark
where we erase borders and pour into each other

The nights; endless journeys through other times
mild awakenings in c-major
the great marine animal of darkness, innumerable arms
embraces that won't let go

We shall live these days, my Love
    arise together and listen
    to the wind beneath the door
    sweeping dreams into the air
    walk the streets without longing
    for other places

My Love, we shall live these days
    with angels, wine and whirling poems
    wander into frost's paradise
    with the sun in our eyes

You Kneel

The world is a bird
flying by
while we reach out our hands
The dream wakes me
and shows
that it means nothing
that we are so far from each other

And you kneel
you are so hard to resist
and you kneel
you are so hard to reach

Life plays
while we despair
for us there's no peace
with hands
restless as moths
flying toward one another
in the darkness
and disappearing

And you kneel
you are so hard to resist
and you kneel
you are so hard to reach

Found on the Beach

Seagulls
back lit
September
in my heart
The waves whisper
autumn to shore

What more can I say
but that I love you
more than I can bear

Sun
between silhouettes of birds
First skies
open first worlds
I remain
and grow smaller
and smaller

On Waiting

I

I am waiting for someone
who whistled beneath my staircase
I am waiting for someone
who brought bread
for distant yearnings
I am waiting for someone
who will never return
I wait
still and forever
no one else
can open the door
to my soul
letting happiness in

II

The candle has burned down
the world stands still
I am waiting for someone
to lie by my side
in the same dream

In the Park

Small and shrivelled
we found it
blue in night's park
eternity lay before us

Trees filled with ocean
ancient echoes in the storm
the wind in the heart
these fossil inscriptions
in the tree's bark
in the innermost chamber of blood

Not far from anywhere
in the world
your hand lay
on my heart

Black Shadow

From the sky's sweeping hand
the bird falls
fishes keep silent in the deepest water

black shadow
against my window
blind eyes watching
mute lips crying
silent songs

black shadow
across my face
in loneliness it writes its longing
into the air
invisible dreams clamour

black shadow
into my life
rivers break inside me
blind wings weeping

At the Window

How much longer
can I live through a memory
of a light rending the dark
How much longer
can I squeeze beauty
from despair
transform stones
into flowers

Out there
you run back and forth
flail your arms
carelessly
about your body
in a savage dance
never looking
over here

I stand at the window
stunned by sorrow

October's Bridges

October somewhere in the world
darkness creeps deeper
through thought's dim passages

it is a rain that looks like asphalt
it is crumbling skeletons of birds
it is large flocks of dreams
drifting away on waves of ashes

October in the wilderness of the soul
the rain drives blood from the core
in the darkest chambers humidity runs
a thick fog down the walls

there is a wind that sweeps sparks
half-quelled into the roaring sea
it is a pure and simple longing for death on bridges
from one kind of darkness to another more dense
it is blue frozen lips
and a black longing for light light light

I have a blue mountain chain

I

I have a blue mountain chain. A series of small hills
that no one calls mountains, but that turn blue
in the evening light.
I think that from these mountains you can see it
all: the valleys to the south and behind the valleys the ocean
and above the ocean the wind that whirls the horizon
further and further away. To the east a city
burning in the dusk.
Also other signs, signs from the universe, dreams'
wonderful cycles, cosmic connections
that cannot be rendered in words and not even in thoughts
but which are always there, always present.
The drizzle in these valleys which leave me to myself
each day and hide the rest from me,
hide the blue mountains, and hide me from myself.

II

I stroll slowly about in my soul
this darkness, this light.
I notice carefully all the details of the labyrinth.
I stroll on twisting paths
as well-known as the streets in my town
or the paths in the garden of my childhood
and yet always new, empty
or inhabited by peculiar meetings
in loneliness, whatever you wish.
Indescribable soul: at times ocean, at times ashes.
This in glimpses incessant traffic between
empty shadows with eyes lost in the void.

III
I have walked here many times, never walked here before.
It is before and in a while and soon I'll reach now.
The landscape stands still. I stand still.
The landscape is eternally moving. I dance motionlessly.
I lay my heart on the ground, ten steps
further ahead I gather it again from the earth
and withered leaves spread all about
as thoughtlessly forgotten poems. Now is once and in a while
in the silence of everything. The heart sings in the wind in the coincidence
of everything for a luminous second.
The wind sings in the heart of wind and blood.
The heart is blue. The heart is air. I fly
with my heart in the wind. The wind sings me into who I am.
Blood and air under a skin of sky. The wind is
everywhere. The wind sings me to everywhere.

from Hjortehjerte
(Deer Heart, 1987)

Silk

purple whisper
silk falls

from your body
of snow and ashes

the room turns
faster on its axis

the air is woven
from the delicate fluttering of wings

cones of sparks
rise at the glistening touch of skin

November

I send you
the frozen presence of my eyes
from rooms
I left
long ago

memory and forgetting
emerge from the same place

I wait here
and die
elsewhere

Scar

laugh while you scratch
your face into my skin

a bloody tattoo
one more scar to love

I dress in ashes
am born in scars

and you make me beautiful

I Came Here to Find You

there were times
I thought
it could still happen
those were days
swaddled in wings

I came here to find you

footsteps through empty streets
to see the gleam of metal
in your eyes
when I darken
into other arms

I came here to find you

hours in silence
in the wild life
loss is a part of everything
always taking leave
the only thing I can give you now
is an open space in which to dance

I came here to find you

and no one likes to return
with matters unfinished
you are deep behind glass, heavy drapes
you spew fire and clothe yourself in snakes
and you never cast a glance
into the dim light of the back room
where I turn around and leave

The Watery Globe

caught
behind fences of breakers
caught
behind walls of beaches
whales whisper
from the forests
of fossilized streams
veins and signs
in the oceans' deserts of water

I slip through the borders of sleep
to approach this
I extend my body's antennae
one second, a lifetime, the beat of a pulse
to receive the smallest signals

caught
in the oceans' freedom
heavenly bodies glide
forward in floating games
tracks across the firmament
from animals showing the way
outward and inward, through to the beginning

my heart is a hydrophone
I listen through the night
through the silence of the ocean
for the deep breath of whales
which keeps the watery globe afloat
in the heart of the weightless blood of the universe

from Skriftsteder
(Scriptures, 1989)

*

faces in the crowd
blinking and shifting,
remain in a glimpse, stop
one by one as clocks in stations
where time ticks and ticks, blink
after blink, second by second,
minute by day by year by life
forever and rushes through
stations in the crowd
where trains no longer leave
where travellers no longer arrive
where lovers no longer recognize
faces in the crowd and rush
toward them like empty living mirrors

*

the water under the stars
we walk across night
each on our own bridge

the days we let lie
crumbling fallow-light
our abandoned shells

birds of burned lime
chained to our hearts
breathe in ever smaller rooms

inhaling the dust
the water under the stars
the stars under the bridges

the bridges under our kisses
these white arms stretched out
like calcified beating wings

*

whom you dream into
your room above the city's black fire
whom you tear apart
in order to gather again with eyes of ashes
whom you write in and out
in and out of each second's white fire

let your nails glow
in my sleep

whom you lead by the hand
across the chipped notes of the floor
whom you send into the night
on behalf of your shady skin
whom you adorn
with open veins–

let your nails glow
in my sleep

whom you crown at the point
of the wildest star
whom you nail onto words
on your door, the cross above the bed, *the moment* –
your smallest movement has an echo
and a shadow in my room

just let your nails
shine their pale moons
throughout the dark
in my sleep

*

for a moment I'm forgotten
a second or less
on a balcony at night
in a strange city
behind the shutters in a room
wedged between rooms
out of a sudden sky
a secret glimpse
or asleep, flakes
falling, melting, evaporating
hidden beneath the sighs

for a moment I forget
for a second or less I disappear
into another shape
released by light
butterfly, a distant contour
an escaping animal-body
the insect eye's vibrating reflection
the stone's heart for nothing
the pulse knocking for no one
a moment, a second or less
pushed deeper into eternity

*

without a single word
let the days stand still
left behind us

the fragrances, the ocean beneath
the earth beneath the ocean
beneath us, the days –
the nights sway back
between the cliffs
behind us

there you say: *you are
so alive*, as if
I could be
and there you hold
your hands over my
face and say
it again: *you are
so alive*, as if
I could be otherwise

without a single word
let the days stand still
the nights between the cliffs
behind us

*

for nothing
this is meant
not as writing
but as a fall from a hidden code
not as skin
but as a whisper
no, not even a whisper
only the sound of a breath
behind a closed door

from At
(To, 1990)

        to walk in a circle
        to fall asleep
        to get lost
        to be shy
        to become

the first night was a lizard
the second night darkness was thick with wings
the third night rain hesitated
the fourth night rain arrived disguised in heavy scents
the fifth night held departure and arrival
the sixth slept calmly
the seventh night opened the dreamer's eyes
the eighth left its mark: seeds and signs
the ninth makes its entrance

the days;
open signs —
my light strikes you
makes you afraid, happy

we speak about space

we rock each other a while

our hands are bowls
we live
in each other's refuge

>   to appear
>   to hold in mind
>   to float
>   to arrive in the world
>   to seek refuge

on this day I am not alone
there is a hand on my shoulder
not a word, not even a whisper
or the sound of breathing
just the weight of this hand
and something waiting
a presence larger than thought
and the shiver
when I don't dare turn around

you died last night
I know from the voices
that broke out of chaos
and took the shape
of cramped bodies
I stood by the window
and saw them run by
hands
covering their faces

        to balance above fear
        to stumble without a place to fall
        to be time's flight toward departure
        to hesitate in the door with leave-taking on the lips
        to look back over the shoulder

was the rain handed down toward you –
did you stand free of the wind –
did the fruit fall into your hands
as only fruit
and did your hands fall
into silence
as only hands –

did the bird's blue root
root in your eyes
or had you already
sensed flight
from your shelter behind the wing –

from Gribbenes Himmel
(Vultures' Sky, 1993)

The Stranger

who is alone, but not lonely
who is complete, but not whole

who carries weight
who finds way

who walks through darkness without fear
who walks still faceless through the dark

who knows who you are, without knowing your name
who stretches out a hand and the hand is open

who lifts a lamp
to see himself in you

Moon Nail

it is under my nails
burning under my nails
these forever setting moons
shiny under my nails
faces forever on their way
through the dark

I will show you loneliness
on a night like this
between my legs

caves beneath the ocean
we take refuge
in each other, frightened fishes
my poor thighs constantly slip
to the sides, slimy plants
grow pale out of the night
we recognize each other's faces
suddenly shiny, white scars in the dark
from another crime

I will show you loneliness
tonight
between my legs

falling
in the abyss of my embrace
your dissolved crystals
a congealed liquid
pulverize every breath
your mouth turns
over the edge of the wound
from a new death

Mad Bird

a small bird by the window
caught in insanity's plumage
attempts over and over
to fly through the glass and into
this image of another life
or is it its own reflection
that gives birth to this eagerness

from where does this mad power spring
did you fly too close to the moon –
what is it you see in the window
which no one else
has yet discovered –

caught from within, peering out
bleeding lips, greedy nails
in my mind I pluck
every single shivering fibre
of this frayed down
and take into possession every one
of insanity's pulse beats

mad bird, lend me
your bruised wings
dress me in your plumage
I don't dream of flight
I only wish to see
the world through your eyes
you seem so convinced
that there is something else
beneath the surface
more worthy of desire

Grandmother

where have I heard
that song before
the cry of chestnuts

where have I seen
that face before – dream
a bright day out
of your darkness!

where does the scent come from
grandmother, you took it
with you into death

now you reach the rain
down towards me
    I cannot receive
now you reach the scent
towards me
    the weight of life
    holds me back

now I glimpse the song
the face behind the rain
nothing remains – everything
returns

your arms long white
you offer the rain
to me, bone-birds
fly from your hands
now I finally hear
silence behind the chestnuts

Carrying Sorrow

today I will carry
my sorrow
down to the sea
perhaps I will
return empty-handed
perhaps I will
not return

the sun lives
without my face
the moon
without my paleness

the trees
without my arms
my arms
which never
reach you

my shadow
has merged with yours
my tongue
is a flake of chalk

your face lives
without my suns
your body
without my moons

today I will carry
my sorrow
down to the sea
perhaps I will
return empty-handed
perhaps I will
never return

Not a Poem

you are a photograph
not a poem
you are an outcast from the sun
not a poem
you are a casting of my heart
not a poem
you are a fossil of something that lacked the strength
to keep the world going
not a poem

the words
remain
leaves
fall from naked branches
the words
shape my lips
into poems
the leaves
make room for a new beginning

the words
remain
the silence
shapes my lips
leaves
falling
from naked branches

Hotel

alone
with bodies that have left
fossilized traces
of life and presence
in this rusty hotel bed
that answers
even the smallest breath

neon flashes against the wall
across the street, flashes the night to pieces
splinters and shards, birds
with eyelids worn thin
beating wildly against the dark

awake here, unravelled
nameless, worldless, in transit
the moon is a wound in the sky

conversations in sealed languages
open up moments to show
that one is no one, but two
contain the possibility
of the dawn

noise from the restaurant
laughter and fragments of music, steps
in the hallway count the distance of seconds
between sudden cracks in the night

I will read a poem
that can lead me further
or just hold me here
in a glimpse, a second
or less
just a small poem –
I too am not
needed here

Exile

my body
is a momentary form
a possible tool
an anchor for something
which is greater
and more important
than me

at the window
now and then
a beam of sunlight
in which I can sit
my soul grasps
gaspingly for heat
near the end of winter

the clouds drag themselves
across mountains, below
forty-eight yellow sheets are hung out
to dry

children's laughter and music
from the closed yards
a ball careening against walls
echoes playing along

I think about butterflies
the light of distant planets, rainbows
and marine forests, teeth
that clench in silence
while nails are ripped out at the roots
in rooms without eyelids

now and then
there is something I understand
momentarily
there is something I can believe in
I never know
with certainty
whether it is god or the devil
living in my body
leading my hand
forever scraping
across page after page
of still
unlived
life

Sloughing

I constantly expect
from this trembling in my lip
that a greater song
will burn along the edge
of my breath

I wait for my body
if nothing else, then a change
of skin, a face beneath
my face, appearing all too
slowly and not yet visible

cells die and make room
for new ones – my blood, seven days
seven years, and it's all over
but unchanged, a sudden
leap toward transformation

is what I want
not a cliff, a new attempt
I just sit, my hand
is heavy, but beats now and then
with the sound of a wing

Travel

maybe
after having travelled
for a long time

you will step into
a silence

maybe
you will know it
like the stones
that whisper
on the bottom of the creek

maybe
you will recognize it
from what you left behind

once

maybe
it doesn't matter
that you no
longer
belong

there is silence
behind the stones
in your hand

from Til
(For, 1995)

Imploding Sky

There are days, even now, that won't move an inch from before. Like today. I stare through windows that are not mine. An imploding sky. I walk through the rooms in an empty house, holding myself as a child by the hand.

My hand, but small. She bites her nails, I can tell. She is someone else, a stranger. I observe her attentively, on the sly. Her experiences will be my memories. I can't remember anything yet. It lies within me somewhere, all that she must go through to get to here. God knows who she will be when she gets that far.

It all lies within me. The moment I want to take it out, want to remember, it is totally empty, a smooth white surface. An imploding sky. I must wait here for her to catch up to me.

The Witness

Does our shadow enter the world before or after us? Is it here already, does it wait in the delivery room? Does it meet us halfway as a stranger, a friend? Or is it incumbent on us to seek it out ourselves – a form, an appointed meeting time in an official envelope, a caretaker, awaiting his toll? Payments with growing interest. A no returns policy. Do we get it handed out like a suit of unmatched clothes from the cleaner's? The sharp creases draw a steep contour against the wall and look like *someone else*. Does it replace the placenta in order to follow us, nurture us, witness us, protect us and carry our dark memories of ourselves? Even in forgetfulness, even at night. Even in the dark a shadow is a shade darker, a mite deeper than the abyss it accompanies.

Entreaty

In a moment when it becomes completely quiet at an intersection in the middle of the day in the busy and scarred part of the city where we stand strange and alone side by side in one of our lives' innumerable repetitions and wait for traffic to yield for signals that flash and a small group with bottles and dogs warble hesitantly on the opposite corner by the cemetery wall and still there are hummingbirds and Siberian tigers somewhere on earth and we suddenly both of us turn our gaze from the asphalt and together in an abrupt vision of the future with our faces turning pale in one and the same direction towards an open window on the fourth floor where a body brusquely lets go of its being and loosens to a fall at the weight of its flesh and the prayer opens its shell of rust and salt and calcium and makes a bridge of light from everyone's lips into heaven while traffic eventually changes direction and we continue on our way on exactly the same course towards what we had intended but we no longer know what is

Thaw

You said you would disguise yourself as a river mouth. That you wanted to be the place where my melted water would eventually run into the ocean. That you would meet me, embrace me there. You said you would embrace me from both shores. You drew it with your hands in the air, your palms open and your fingers braided together. You took me and held me tightly like a body of water, long and hard, like the power of water. Both from the front and from behind like you said you would, from both shores. That was what you wanted. Your look changed to a wild darkness, revealed just vaguely under the heavy wings of your eyelids. And I gave in to you, gave in and received you with a sudden song from the depths. I gave in again and again, the hairy back of your hand, the bend in your neck and its pitch like when one gives in to the wind that tears the last yellow leaves from the trees after winter's gone. Like one gives in to the thaw that drives the spring river violently down the mountain, and you lose your footing crossing the ford.

Photography

Late in the afternoon the colours become visible again. They regain themselves after the glossy light we have moved through. Like something that had to be overcome, a fever without memory. Like clean sheets of paper we arrive in the afternoon. Our names deserted, empty shells, uninhabited. The low lying sun makes us look happy. We don't know if we're still the same. We don't know if we still love each other. In this way a few more minutes will pass.

In the Old City
a fragment

I sit in a car with my father. We eat raw meat from a plastic tray. Pork chops. He says it's something I have to learn. That in my life I must be able to eat raw meat. In case. Like now. It is almost flavourless. It's the sensation between your fingers, your teeth. I won't recognize that sensation till much later in life.

In the Desert

Suddenly something happened. We had been travelling on this train through the night, for hours, and now it was late morning. A loud banging tore us from the journey's torpor. It sounded like stones hurled against the undercarriage. Just beneath our feet. Through the floor we could feel the thumping. It persisted. The train slowed down and stopped laboriously. When it came to a complete halt, and once again we could hear the silence, we stepped out to see what had caused the noise.

We were in the middle of the desert. The sun was already high in the sky, burning the horizon into a distant shimmer. As far as the eye could see there was not a soul in sight. Only a few dry bushes stood out in the vast landscape.

The carcass of a horse was caught under our carriage. The body of the animal had been torn, violently, fiercely: its hind part missing. Intestines hung from the belly in large glistening clusters. Everted lips exposed a frozen grin. Its eyes were staring at something far in the distance. Nothing could release this image from my retina: its hooves, which had been striking against the undercarriage as they dragged across the ties, running wildly into death.

Days

Where is my life going? I don't know myself. It is afternoon. I try to make myself light to keep up.

Days slip through the mesh in the net. Nothing or almost nothing adheres. Totally white, utterly glossy days, without faces, without voices.

The pen I put down on the kitchen table wrote, 'Life after this must begin somewhere.' That was several weeks ago. My attention does not stretch further than the hand that fills the glass and the hand that lifts the glass to the lips.

Nothing is forever, nothing, and that is how I want it. To slip through the mesh in the net and slide into the sea.

From Kamikaze
(1999)

THE MOON KNOWS
and my blood

hospital-white nights of vigil
we are both in the world
turning on an axis
of displaced images
we each cross a border
and look into each other
through layer upon layer of sky
an unending space
entrenched

your eyes
so blue

you climb a ladder
without foothold or end

the moon knows
and my blood

signals whirr in the air
I fan away instincts
insects drawn
by dark veins
swelling
from my skin

in order to reach you, meet you
wrap you in the homage of my pulse

when promises
prayers and spells
no longer
can hold you here

I REFUSE to accept
the spine's dictated script
which at the precise moment
lets itself dissolve, lets itself be inserted
as a footnote of terror
in the great law
that has condemned us to carry
the quake's loosening
when the alibi doesn't hold
and the body surrenders itself
when dawn cleans up
among the stars

YOU KNOW THOSE NIGHTS
your cheek pales in memory
of the love you didn't give
the impression of the hand
that offers the morning light
to you
and is never seen

it catches you from within
it wants you – nothing else
but the way in which you now
turn in your sleep
and reach for your cheek

If I SAY that white horses
white coffins, white sheets lash in the wind
that you walk about in there
in a room I glimpse
behind a door that springs open and open
the further in I go
if I say that white pages
chalk-white pages and more white pages
rip the air and I hold
all the blood necessary
to write a life
but I have no hands

YOUR NAME IS WRITTEN
on a torn slip
of a pink envelope
pushed into a wallet
left on a bridge

a woman calls
and leaves the message
in the moist folds
of her voice
her words
are fungus spores
the wind drives in
through the crack
to another life
where I deny
who I am
to someone who seeks me
in a strange place

I am
nailed to the circle of the present
with an exact knowledge
of the cone of light
that drills its way into
a rigid pupil
in the room without eyelids
where all death awaits
redemption

FROM NOW ON I will always
prefer chaos
dancing, maimed insects
caught in a dusty column
of sunlight

always prefer
insanity's shrill branching
that wedges
into day's ground

sulphureous glimpses flare up
and crash
a cascade
of splintered glances

reason burns bridges
behind me – go ahead and carry
wood for this bonfire!

always grasp in blindness
for what cannot be reached
always prefer
a depraved possibility
that could cost me
my life or what
is worse

climb towards heaven
jubilantly chaotic
on a dusty column
of sunlight

New Poems

Birthday at the Assistens Cemetery

Any day at all.
A Wednesday perhaps, but this day
the sun melted into honey amber,
it was the day of my third decade,
a red letter day at the threshold
to the life ahead. That which
is mine and I fall asleep
in an untimely satiation of days on the nearest
lawn – a delicately flowered meadow in the middle
of the city's carbon dioxide-steaming asphalt.
At the cemetery, as it happened
where the earth is fertilized forever.

Here sleep is sweet, in good
company, and deep – it sinks
quickly like a glass anchor
into the spinal cord's bottomless depths.
The dream's path but a whisper, a chalk dry
whistling from bones and dust.
It tempts and hovers. I don't feel
the insects and worms that test
the topography of my body, its
smells, its salty moist creases.
Its untested possibilities.
An inspection of antennae.
Tentacles walk, measure,
note, let the dream see myself
through faceted eyes, my multiplicity
fairly distributed among worms,
maggots and microbes. Just a cool
vibration in a contented rest, a
childhood. As a prayer forever

and again. The liquid beneath the tongue
waters the earth, a prayer for resurrection
as a column of rain.

But whose is the scratching nail
with a rim of dirt, the coarse finger
that suddenly gnaws at my shoulder?
A sexton, death's gardener with
subterranean powers – to wake
the dead and banish them
from paradise. A merciless border guard
laying the wall of separation harshly in place:
'No one may lie here!'
Still young and smuttily lounging
in a limp eel of a dress
around my waist and thighs, that glisten
in the sunlight, break into life's
portal and wake the living juices
till they rise. Supported by a spade
he stands and stares deeply into my sex!

Wide awake so suddenly that I'm blinded
by the world of the living, the original scream
echoes dumbly in a tightening
of the lip until the pupil finds
a suitable crack and realizes on
which flower meadow in June
my nap took place. The earth –
the one for the living – almost indistinguishable
from paradise for a split second.
But no one may lie here.
'Here ashes are to be spread.'

The realization hits my body
with a glowing arrow, digs
in – not yet thwarted,
not yet dust and memory
I must immediately leave my resting place
of sweet dreams, my death,
and return to the rubble,
the crumbling mortar, to the life
ahead. That which is mine.

Death sank in its yellow teeth,
took a bite but found my flesh
too tart and spat it out, jeering
that I had to hang a little longer,
a hook in my flesh, and aging. Instead
it took a much stronger link
from the chain of my blood and let me
dangle in the abattoir,
still alive.

The Pattern of Dead Insects

The pattern of dead insects
on the windowsill
carries traces of a woman
who stood there
and loosened her hair.

It is said about her
that she was reckless.
That she made herself accessible.
That without resistance she let the moon
visit every moist fold
and did not retreat
when the sky penetrated.

That her eyes beamed
and her lips parted,
glossy, and ever so lightly,
when she was forsaken.

Every tear
has an open window.
Every tear
has a sun and six planets

Scratched in the surface
of a stray hair
is a map of the web of galaxies,
of paths, that shows the place
that fate
leads to,

and who can tell
the cry of surrender
from the one tinged with hope?

The Cannibals

Not a ripple across the lips.
It is said without the slightest hesitation:
every new child is a hope for the world,
but look who's speaking with a hungry mouth.
Every child – a new surface to fill
with fear to the skin's trembling limit,
to violate in the name of love's caress
with the rainbow as airtight alibi.

A biological naïveté populates the world
with still more mouths to feed.
Ever more small silken bodies to pierce
on the ego's lance, and to grill
over the ice blue flame of the self.
The shadows on the wall search, flutter in vain
to imitate the heart of grace.

Now they have fed, they have copulated, emptied
themselves into each other. Now my progenitor
sleeps in fragile shells, my dear flock
with dripping chins and stomachs rumbling
with digestion's chemistry. The small tucks
in heavy bodies – imagine, they manage
to awake a puffed-up tenderness
when you in the gleam of moonlight observe
somnambulant hands wave demons
away, like tireless flies.

I watch alone and await
regeneration in flapping shreds
of meat, where chunks are missing
after their orgy on my body.
And I am amazed that my throat,
even in a stranglehold, can only utter
love in answer to this mistake
that I was born and exist, yes, I *am*
and carry proudly evolution's crown of creation,
embrace bodily an inner jungle
of continuity and possible completion.

I am, yes, and I carry in each
distant cell, in each sighing capillary
a sounding cry for generation
and repetition of features and defects
and stumbling steps into the future.
Even I rock in this hour from side
to side to the rhythm of longing's instinct:
let me see my blood's descending link
with innocent eyes and angels' hair, a little
cannibal – oh, give me a mouth to feed
with flaws and wants. Give me beauty's
resonant string, set in motion by a coupling.

Tonight all men are my husband
and all women his wife. All children
are my offspring and all offspring my progenitor
floating directionless and alone
while I keep watch and boil over
from witch's milk in swollen breasts, infected
by jeering insomnia. Here hope lives
in tight quarters, but the dancing place
is wide open for infatuation and promises
going astray in the shrub of genes.
On earth more are living
in dubious consent than those
who have ever turned their backs on the orgy.
The family's holy cannibalism
ends only when everyone has eaten
and I am still hungry!

Author Biography

Ulrikka S. Gernes was born in Sweden to Danish parents. Her father, Poul Gernes, was one of Denmark's most famous visual artists and a professor at the Royal Academy of Fine Arts. While working with her father, Ulrikka was trained as a mural painter. Ulrikka finished high school in 1984. Instead of continuing her formal education, she travelled widely, particularly in Europe and Asia. She lived in Hong Kong for six years, working as a freelance editor and translator. For the past three years Ulrikka has been living in Copenhagen. In addition to her freelance work, she is now the Chair of the Gernes Foundation, a foundation created after her father's death. This Foundation gives grants to young artists. She also continues to work on visual art projects such as works for exhibitions and murals. As a poet she has published nine collections of poetry. Ulrikka also does readings and performances both on her own and with jazz artists. She has written radio essays, and other radio work, for the National Radio of Denmark.

Translators' Biographies

Per Brask is a writer, dramaturg and translator. He is Professor of Theatre and Drama at the University of Winnipeg. He has directed plays in several theatres in Montreal and Winnipeg. Per has also published poetry, short stories, drama, translations, interviews and articles in numerous journals such as *Anthropologica, Canadian Theatre Review, Danish Literary Magazine, Descant, Malahat Review,* and *Performing Arts Journal.* He has written for the stage, radio and television. Among his books are *Duets* (with George Szanto, Coteau, 1989), *Aboriginal Voices: Amerindian, Inuit and Sami Theatre* (ed. with William Morgan, Johns Hopkins University Press, 1992), *God's Blue Morris: a Selection of Poems by Niels Hav* (edited and translated with Patrick Friesen. Crane Editions, 1993), and *Essays on Kushner's Angels* (ed., Blizzard Publishing, 1995).

Patrick Friesen has worked in a variety of writing genres and teaches creative writing at Kwantlen University College in Vancouver. Among his poetry publications are *A Broken Bowl* (Brick Books, 1997), *St. Mary at Main* (The Muses' Company, 1998), and *Carrying the Shadow* (Beach Holme Books, 1999). His work has been carried in more than a dozen anthologies. His plays include *The Shunning* (Prairie Theatre, 1985) and *The Raft* (Prairie Theatre Exchange, 1992). Patrick has collaborated on several translations of Danish poetry with Per Brask. He has also worked with composers such as Cate Friesen and Marilyn Lerner, and has written text for modern dance. Patrick has frequently written for CBC Radio.